TRAINS

by Anne Rockwell

E. P. Dutton • New York

for Pyke

**Published in the United States by
E. P. Dutton, a division of
Penguin Books USA Inc.**

Published simultaneously in Canada by
Fitzhenry & Whiteside Limited, Toronto

Editor: Ann Durell

Printed in Hong Kong by South China Printing Co.
First Edition   W   10 9 8 7 6 5 4 3 2

Library of Congress Cataloging-in-Publication Data
Rockwell, Anne F.
  Trains / by Anne Rockwell.—1st ed.
    p.   cm.
  Summary: Simple text and illustrations introduce a
variety of trains and their uses. Includes freight trains,
passenger trains, monorails, and subways.
  ISBN 0-525-44377-0
  1. Railroads—Juvenile literature.
[1. Railroads—Trains.]   I. Title
TF148.R63   1988   87-22180
625.1—dc19   CIP
                                          AC

There are toy trains

and real trains.

Trains go on tracks.

Engineers drive the locomotives
that pull the cars along the tracks.

Signals tell the engineer to stop or go.

Passenger trains carry people.

Freight trains carry things.

Subways are trains that go below

the streets of big cities.

Elevated railroads have trains that go

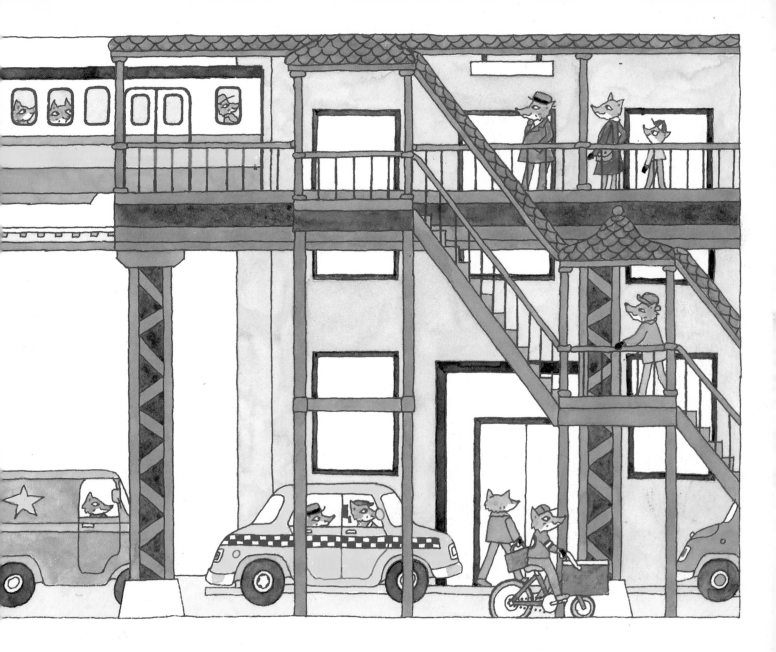

above the streets of big cities.

A monorail goes on a one-rail track

and has wheels you cannot see.

Old trains had steam engines.

Now train locomotives have diesel engines

when they travel across the countryside.

Now trains use electric power lines

when they come into a big city.

My electric train goes around the living room.
Here it comes—out of the tunnel!